_____ *✍*
Presented To

_____ *✍*
From

_____ *✍*
Date

SUNSET WITH GOD

PORTABLE GIFT EDITION

Honor Books
Tulsa, Oklahoma

Sunset with God, *portable gift edition*
ISBN 1-56292-554-7
Copyright © 1998 by Honor Books
P.O. Box 55388
Tulsa, Oklahoma 74155

Drawn from original manuscript prepared by W. B. Freeman Concepts, Inc.
Tulsa, Oklahoma.

Cover illustration by Taylor Bruce.

REFERENCES

INTRODUCTION

By the end of the day, most of us are completely exhausted. Our bodies are tired, our energy is depleted, and our minds are empty. Creative ideas, workable solutions, and wise answers are nowhere to be found. Our emotions are frayed, and our ability to communicate and relate to others is almost nonexistent.

We may be teetering on the edge. At that point, we are desperate for a place in which to refresh and rejuvenate—a place to once again find ourselves.

In the midst of your weariness, take time for the Lord. Don't shut Him out, thinking that prayer or devotional time is just "one more thing" to schedule into your day. Embrace your time with Him as a life-giving respite.

Tonight, trust the Lord to pour Himself into you, filling you to overflowing with His divine presence. God will infuse you with His strength, His power, His wisdom, His love—His life! You'll go to bed feeling full and whole. God is your sufficiency—He is all you need for every area of your life. There is none like Him!

THE POWER OF PRAYER

⤷ BECAUSE EVENING is wind-down time, we may think our prayers will lack the power and conviction that is available earlier in the day. However, prayer at any time of the day can have a powerful effect on our world. For instance:

- Queen Mary said she feared the prayers of John Knox more than she feared all the armies of Scotland.

- John Wesley's prayers brought revival to England, sparing them the horrors of the French Revolution.

- Revival spread throughout the colonies when Jonathan Edwards prayed.

Time after time, history has been shaped by prayer. Rev. Billy Graham says, "We have not yet learned that a man can be more powerful on his knees than behind the most powerful weapons that can be developed."[1]

Matthew 14:23 tells us that Jesus sought to be alone with the Father after what must have been an extremely taxing day of preaching, teaching, and healing the multitudes. Perhaps our prayers are *more* powerful when weariness causes us to drop the pretenses of pretty language in favor of direct communication with God, into Whose hands we've placed our lives.

> *And when he [Jesus] had sent the multitudes away,*
> *he went up into a mountain apart to pray:*
> *and when the evening was come, he was there alone.*
> —MATTHEW 14:23 KJV

EVENING AND MORNING

FROM THE Hebrew perspective, the day begins at *evening*, specifically with the setting of the sun. How unlike our Western tradition, where we start our days at the crack of dawn and consider night to be the *end* of a long day.

So, what does it mean for the day to begin at evening?

For Hebrew people through the centuries, the transition from afternoon to evening has been marked by prayer. After prayer, families gather together for a meal. After the evening meal, they gather together to read and study God's commandments. The evening ends in rest.

It was only *after* a Hebrew talked with God, enjoyed the love and fellowship of family, studied the Scripture, and rested, that work was undertaken!

What would happen in your life if you adopted this strategy for your evening hours? Is it possible that you would find yourself more renewed and refreshed?

Why not give it a try? Begin your next day in the evening, and wake up knowing you're not just beginning; you're reaching the completion of a full and productive day! ✍

And there was evening, and there was morning—the first day.
—GENESIS 1:5

COME HOME

❧ ONCE THERE was a widow who lived in a miserable attic with her son. Years before, the woman had married against her parents' wishes and had gone to live in a foreign land with her husband.

Her husband had proved irresponsible and unfaithful, and after a few years he died without having made any provision for her and their child.

The happiest times in the child's life were when the mother took him in her arms and told him about her father's house in the old country. The child had never seen his grandfather's home, but to him it was the most beautiful place in all the world.

One day the postman knocked at the attic door. The mother recognized the handwriting on the envelope he brought, and with trembling fingers broke the seal. There was a check and a slip of paper with just two words: "Come home."[2]

Like this father, our Heavenly Father opens His arms to receive us. The Father is calling you to come home. Why not finish your day in the comfort and provision of His presence?

For this son of mine was dead and is alive again;
he was lost and is found.
—LUKE 15:24

NIGHT WATCH

  VÁCLAV HAVEL is a former president of what used to be Czechoslovakia. In 1948 the Communists took power in his country. From that time, Havel was part of a defiant underground that opposed the Soviet government.

In 1970, several U.S. senators met with Havel. They brought what they thought would be good news. They told him they intended to press for legislation that would allow dissidents like himself to emigrate to the West.

"What good would that do?" Havel asked. "Only by staying here and struggling here can we ever hope to change things."[3]

Times of trial and struggle often seem like long, dark nights. But doing the right thing—even if it's the hard thing—is cause for hope. How do we maintain those long night watches when there seems little change in our circumstances?

Placing your hope in the Lord helps you to go on. He will lead you and guide your steps. He will remove your mountains. He will strengthen you, helping you to be patient. And He will open your eyes to His works all around you. 🐟

You are my hope, O Lord GOD.
—PSALM 71:5 NKJV

LEAVE IT TO ME

❦ MARY ELLEN, a Christian woman, once had a great burden in her life. She was in danger of jeopardizing her physical and emotional health and was on the verge of a nervous breakdown. She recognized, however, that there wasn't anything *she* could do to change her circumstances.

Then Mary Ellen came across a story in a magazine about another woman, Connie, who like herself, had major difficulties in her life. In the account, a friend asked Connie how she was able to bear up under the load of such troubles. Connie replied, "I take my problems to the Lord, but we must not only *take* our problems there. We must *leave* our problems with the Lord."

Mary Ellen realized she had not failed to *take* her problems to the Lord, but she had failed to *leave* them with Him.

The Lord wants you to cast your burdens on Him. He desires for you to give Him your problems, leave them with Him, and go on with life in full confidence that He will take care of those things you have trusted to Him.

Cast your burden on the Lord [releasing the weight of it]
and He will sustain you.
—PSALM 55:22 AMP

QUALITY TIME

IN HIS book *Unto the Hills*, Billy Graham tells a story about a little girl and her father who were great friends and enjoyed spending time together.

Then one day, the father noticed a change in his daughter. If he went for a walk, she excused herself from going. Knowing that she was growing up, he rationalized that she must be expected to lose interest in her daddy as she made other friends. Nevertheless, her absence grieved him deeply, and he was not in a particularly happy mood on his birthday. Later that day, his daughter presented him with a pair of exquisitely worked slippers.

At last he understood and said, "My darling, I like these slippers very much, but next time buy the slippers and let me have you all the days. I would rather have my child than anything she can make for me."

Is it possible that our Heavenly Father sometimes feels lonely for the company of His children? Take a walk with your Heavenly Father as the sun sets. You will be blessed and so will He! ✍

Thou wilt shew me the path of life: in thy presence is fulness of joy.
—PSALM 16:11 KJV

EARLY TO BED

MOST OF us are familiar with the old saying:

> Early to bed and early to rise,
> Makes a man healthy and wealthy and wise.

Research has shown that sufficient sleep is the foremost factor in a person's ability to sustain a high performance level, cope with stress, and feel a sense of satisfaction in life. Sufficient sleep directly impacts our moods and emotions, our ability to think creatively and to respond quickly, and our ability to sustain work or exertion. It is as vital to our health as what we eat and drink.

More good news about sleep is that every hour of sleep we get before midnight is twice as beneficial as the hours after midnight!

A good night's sleep is one of God's blessings to you. Sufficient sleep was a part of His design for your body and His plan for your life. When you make it a habit to retire early, you put yourself in a position to receive this blessing, which makes it easier to rise early and seek the Lord for wisdom and strength for the day ahead.

O God, You are my God; early will I seek You.
—Psalm 63:1 NKJV

THE NIGHT SKY

〜 WHEN WAS the last time you gazed up into the star-filled sky on a clear night? Jamie Buckingham described a night like that in the snowy mountains of North Carolina:

I walked up the dark, snow-covered road toward Cowee Bald. The sky had cleared, revealing a billion stars twinkling in the clear, cold night. The only sound was the gurgling of a small mountain stream beside the road and the soft crunch of my shoes in the snow. All the other night noises were smothered, leaving me with the impression of standing alone on earth.

I remembered a quote from the German philosopher, Kant. Something about two irrefutable evidences of the existence of God: the moral law within and the starry universe above. I breathed His name: "God."

Then, overwhelmed by His presence, I called Him what I had learned to call Him through experience: "Father!"[4]

Tonight, contemplate the stars in the heavens. You will find there a hint of eternity. What an awesome thought that the Creator of such vastness invites you to a *personal* relationship as His child.

> *I consider Thy heavens, the work of Thy fingers,*
> *the moon and the stars, which Thou hast ordained.*
> —PSALM 8:3 NAS

TRUE RICHES

THEY WERE married as soon as they graduated from college. Within two decades, they had reached some pretty lofty rungs on the ladder of success.

Then one day, the bottom dropped out of this couple's life. This "Couple-Who-Had-It-All" started down the road to becoming the "Couple-Who-Lost-It-All." In the midst of their problems, the police came to their door late one night to tell them their oldest son had been killed in a car accident.

This couple discovered something vitally important in the course of putting their lives back together. A neighbor invited them to church and thinking that they had nothing to lose by going, they started attending, eventually becoming regular members. To their amazement, they found they were enjoying Bible study, making lots of genuine friends, and feeling accepted for who they were— not for what they had in the way of material possessions.[5]

Ideally, none of us will have to lose it all in order to find it all. Keeping our priorities straight, remembering to put God first, and others ahead of ourselves is the key! ✍

Don't store up treasures on earth!
—MATTHEW 6:19 CEV

GET UNDERSTANDING

❧ IN A sociological study, fifty people over the age of ninety-five were asked the question: "If you could live your life over again, what would you do differently?" This was one woman's response:

I'd make more mistakes next time; I'd relax; I would limber up; I would be sillier than I have been this trip; I would take fewer things seriously; I would take more chances; I would perhaps have more actual troubles, but I'd have fewer imaginary ones.

You see, I'm one of those people who lives sensibly and sanely hour after hour, day after day. Oh, I've had my moments, and if I had it to do over again, I'd have more of them, instead of living so many years ahead of time.

If I had to do it again, I would travel lighter than I have. If I had my life to live over, I would start barefoot earlier in the spring and stay that way later in the fall. I would go to more dinners; I would ride more merry-go-rounds; I would pick more daisies.

Listen and learn.

Incline your ear to wisdom, and apply your heart to understanding.
—PROVERBS 2:2 NKJV

EVERYDAY NEEDS

❧ "OH, NO! We're going to have to run for the ferry again!" Elaine cried. "And, unless we find a parking place in the next minute or two, we're never going to make it!"

"I told you we needed to get away from your office sooner," her daughter, Cathy, chided. "You just can't count on finding a parking place within walking distance of the ferry when the waterfront is full of summer tourists and conventioneers!"

Elaine prayed aloud, "Lord, we'll circle this block one more time. Please have someone back out or we're not going to make it."

"Mom, there it is!" Cathy shouted. "I have to admit—sometimes you have a lot more faith than I do. Who'd think God would be interested in whether or not we find a parking place?"

"But that's the exciting part of it," she explained. "God is interested in every part of our lives!"[6]

The Lord knows all the circumstances of your day and your tomorrow. Trust Him to be the "Lord of the details." 🌿

This is the confidence we have in approaching God: that if we ask anything according to his will, he hears us. And if we know that he hears us— whatever we ask—we know that we have what we asked of him.
—1 JOHN 5:14-15

29

SATISFACTION

❧ "SATISFACTION GUARANTEED" promise the ads for a new car, a refreshing soft drink, or a vacation at an exotic resort. There is no end to the commercial world's promises of fulfilled hopes and dreams.

Would you describe our culture as satisfied?

If you answer "no," you're not alone. Author Max Lucado doesn't think so either. He said, "That is one thing we are not. We are not satisfied. . . ."

Satisfaction is hard to obtain. We are promised fulfillment many times a day, but the promises seem empty especially after we have "taken the bite."[7]

There is nothing on earth that can satisfy our deepest longing. In *Mere Christianity*, C. S. Lewis wrote: "If I find in myself a desire which no experience in this world can satisfy, the most probable explanation is that I was made for another world." We *were* made for another world—Heaven! The desire for satisfaction is very strong. However, Scripture tells us that there is only one thing that will satisfy: "I shall be satisfied when I awake in Your likeness" (Psalm 17:15 NKJV). 🌿

In Your presence is fullness of joy.
—PSALM 16:11 NKJV

31

HIS PROMISE OF PEACE

∞ A WOMAN who grew up on a large farm fondly remembers some special times with her father:

During the winter months, Dad didn't have to work as hard and long as he did the rest of the year. . . . He never refused my bid to climb up on his lap. Often, he would read to me, or invite me to read a story to him. Other times, we didn't talk at all. We just gazed at the fire and enjoyed the warmth of our closeness.

As I grew, I thought it odd that other kids dreaded the "indoor" days of winter. For me they meant the incredible pleasure of having my father very nearly all to myself.

Just as winter is God's season of rest for Earth, we sometimes experience "winter" in our spiritual lives. Like children who dread "indoor days," we can feel stifled and penned in by these spiritual winters.

Why not use these times to snuggle close to the Heavenly Father and listen to His gentle voice of love and comfort? ☙

Be still, and know that I am God.
—PSALM 46:10 KJV

33

CRADLED

∽ A NUMBER of years ago, two young women boarded a ferry to cross the English Channel. About halfway through their journey, the ferry hit rough waters.

When it became apparent that the pitching of the boat was not going to abate, one of the women decided to return to her seat in the middle of the ferry. She soon fell asleep and experienced no more seasickness. Toward the end of the trip, after the ferry had moved into calmer waters, the other woman joined her.

"That was *awful*," she exclaimed. "I was nauseous for two hours!"

"I'm sorry to hear that," said the second woman.

"Weren't you sick?" the first woman asked in amazement. "No," her friend admitted. "I simply imagined myself being rocked in the arms of God, and I fell asleep."

All around you today, life may be unsettled and stormy. But when you return to the "center" of your life, the Lord, He will set you in safety. Trust Him to bring you through the rough waters to the place He has prepared for you.

Now will I arise, saith the LORD;
I will set him in safety from him that puffeth at him.
—PSALM 12:5 KJV

HE KEEPS US SINGING

∾ EVANGELIST AND singer N. B. Vandall had no idea his life was about to change. Suddenly, one of his sons rushed into the house crying, "Paul is hurt! A car hit him!"

Vandall found his son at a nearby hospital. The surgeon did not offer much hope for him to live.

He went home to give his family a report. Then, he returned to the living room and fell on his knees to pray, but the words wouldn't come. Vandall went to the piano and in minutes, wrote a hymn titled "After."

> After the toil and the heat of the day,
> After my troubles are past,
> After the sorrows are taken away,
> I shall see Jesus at last. . . .
> He will welcome me home—
> After the day is through."

Paul had an almost-perfect recovery from his injuries.[8]

Like Vandall, we can be thankful when God comes to us in the midst of our tribulations. When we turn our focus from our struggles back to God, we can see His awesome power to overcome whatever we may be facing.

He put a new song in my mouth, a song of praise to our God.
Many will see and fear, and put their trust in the Lord.
—PSALM 40:3 NRSV

TIGHTROPE TRUST

IN THE mid-nineteenth century, tightrope walker Blondin stretched a two-inch steel cable across Niagara Falls. As he did, a large crowd gathered to watch. He asked the onlookers, "How many of you believe that I can carry the weight of a man across this gorge?"

The growing crowd shouted and cheered, believing that he could perform this difficult feat. Then Blondin asked, "How many of you believe that I can actually carry a person across the gorge?" Again, the crowd cheered him on.

"Which one of you will climb on my shoulders and let me carry you across the Falls?" Silence fell across the crowd.

Finally, a volunteer came forward. Who was this person? It was Blondin's manager. As they prepared to cross the Falls, Blondin said, "You must not trust your own feelings, but mine. If you trust your feelings, we will both fall." They made it across to the other side safely.

Jesus gives us the same instructions when we are asked to trust Him in difficult circumstances: "Don't trust your own feelings, trust Me to carry you through."

I know whom I have believed, and am persuaded that he is able to keep that which I have committed unto him against that day.
—2 TIMOTHY 1:12 KJV

FRAGMENTS

🕯 MARGARET BROWNLEY tells of her son's first letters from camp:

I received the first letter from him three days after he left for camp. The childish scrawl read: "Camp is fun, but the food is yucky!" The next letter offered little more: "Jerry wet the bed." *Who's Jerry?* I wondered. The third and final letter had this interesting piece of news: "The nurse said it's not broken."

It made me think of my own sparse messages to God. "Dear Lord," I plead when a son is late coming home, "keep him safe." Or, "Give me strength."

Are my messages to God as unsatisfactory to Him as my son's letters were to me? With a guilty start, I realized that it had been a long time since I'd had a meaningful chat with the Lord.

When my son came home, he told me all about his adventures. It was good to have him home and safe. "Thank-you, God," I murmured, and then caught myself. It was time I sent God more than just a hasty note from "camp."[9]

One day Jesus was praying in a certain place. When he finished, one of his disciples said to him, "Lord, teach us to pray."
—LUKE 11:1

UNIQUELY FASHIONED

   AS YOU lie in bed tonight, stretch your limbs in all directions and then relax for a moment to ponder the fact that your body has been fearfully and wonderfully made. When you stop to think about all the intricate details involved in the normal functioning of your body—just one creation among countless species and organisms on the planet—you must conclude, "The Designer of *this* piece of work had a marvelous plan."

The Lord Who knows precisely *how* you were made, also knows *why* He made you. When something in your life goes amiss, He knows how to fix it. When you err or stray from His commandments, He knows how to woo you back and work all things together so something good can come out of even the worst tragedies and mistakes.

You have been uniquely fashioned for a specific purpose. He has a "design" for your life. It is His own imprint, His own mark. Resolve in these night hours to be true to what the Lord has made you to be and to become.

I will praise thee; for I am fearfully and wonderfully made; marvellous are thy works; and that my soul knoweth right well.
—PSALM 139:14 KJV

ALL THE DETAILS

❧ IT WAS Saturday morning and Andrea was feeling crushed under a mounting pile of pressures. In the midst of her turmoil, her son Steven's Sunday school teacher called. "Is Steven going to the carnival with us this afternoon?"

"He didn't mention anything about it."

"If he didn't bring home his permission slip, just write the usual information on a slip of paper and send it with him."

44

Andrea was just pulling a cake from the oven when she heard the doorbell ring followed by an awful commotion. "I can't go!" Steven wailed. "I don't have one of those pink papers!"

"Oh, yes you do. Only yours happens to be white," she said as she dried his tears, stuffed the paper in his pocket, and sent him out the door.

Back in the kitchen Andrea wondered, "Hasn't he been my child long enough to know I'd have a solution?" Suddenly a smile crept across her face, she could almost hear her Heavenly Father say, "Haven't you been My child long enough to know that I have it all taken care of?"[10]

Do not let your hearts be troubled.
Trust in God; trust also in me.
—JOHN 14:1

DEAL WITH IT!

 ANGER IS not a bad thing. It energizes us to action, to right the wrong, to defend the innocent. But too often, anger is expressed in inappropriate, destructive ways. We can fly off the handle and act in ways that are as hurtful as what caused us to be angry in the first place. An old proverb says, "He who goes angry to bed has the devil for a bedfellow."

There are several things we can do to take control of our anger before it takes control of us:

1. Don't be overly sensitive and interpret everything as a personal affront to you.

2. Pray about your attitudes and responses to situations that make you angry.

3. Put the energy generated by your anger to good use in reaching out to correct injustice and resolve conflict. Direct the focus of your anger away from yourself and other people to the problems that are causing it.[11]

Whatever the source of your anger, deal with it—and put it to good use. God can turn *anything* around to work for your good. ✒

Be ye angry, and sin not.
—EPHESIANS 4:26 KJV

CALMING DOWN

❧ DO YOU sometimes feel as if you spent the day pushing a boulder up a mountain with a very small stick? Memorize these words:

I lift up my eyes to the hills—where does my help come from?
My help comes from the LORD, the Maker of heaven and earth.
—PSALM 121:1-2

Are you worried about making mistakes or letting your family down? Memorize these words:

He will not let your foot slip—he who watches over you will not slumber;
indeed, he who watches over Israel will neither slumber nor sleep.
—PSALM 121:3-4

Does unnecessary anxiety sometimes get the best of you? Memorize these words:

The LORD watches over you—the LORD is your shade at your right hand;
the sun will not harm you by day, nor the moon by night.
—PSALM 121:5-6

You have just memorized over half a psalm! Now, memorize the rest and repeat it to yourself every night. Personalize it. Then rest in the knowledge that God has you, your life, and the rest of the universe under control.

My sleep had been pleasant to me.
—JEREMIAH 31:26

UNIQUELY POSITIONED

IMAX FILMMAKERS once produced a movie titled *Cosmos*. In it, they explored the "edges" of creation—both outer space as viewed through the most powerful telescope, and inner space as viewed through the most powerful microscope. At the far reaches of space, clumps of matter (huge stars) seem to be suspended in fixed motion and separated by vast areas of seemingly empty blackness.

The same can be said for the depths of inner space. Both inner and outer space appear as if they may very well extend into infinity.

In contrast, the created earth is suspended between these two poles. Our world is filled with varied colors, dynamic forms, differing patterns, and changing seasons.

It is as if God has placed man at the very center of His vast creation. We are "hung in the balance" literally, as well as figuratively.

We are specially *positioned* in God's creation. And the Lord has a place for you specifically. Thank God for your uniqueness today. Praise Him for all that He has designed you to be, to become, and to give. 🦢

> *When I consider your heavens, the work of your fingers,*
> *the moon and the stars, which you have set in place,*
> *what is man that you are mindful of him?*
> —PSALM 8:3-4

AGE IS AN ATTITUDE

HELEN KELLER was once asked how she would approach old age. She responded: "Age seems to be only another physical handicap, and it excites no dread in me."

She continued:

Once I had a dear friend of eighty, who impressed upon me the fact that he enjoyed life more than he had done at twenty-five. "Never count how many years you have, as the French say," he would insist, "but how many interests you have. Do not stale your days by taking for granted the people about you, or the things which make up your environment, and you will ever abide in a realm of fadeless beauty."

It is as natural for me, certainly, to believe that the richest harvest of happiness comes with age as that true sight and hearing are within, not without.

Years before we reach "old age" we determine whether that time will be a gracious and pleasant time or a time when we rehearse life's hurts with bitterness. The attitudes with which we invest our days now will characterize the days of our senior years. 🖋

The righteous flourish like the palm tree. . . .
They still bring forth fruit in old age.
—PSALM 92:12,14 RSV

NOT EXACTLY PUPPY LOVE

AARON AND Abbey had been happily married for nearly a year when Aaron bought Abbey a "present" she never wanted: a great big Chow puppy with paws the size of baseballs.

"Pup," as he came to be called, won an uneasy spot in their household. Pup sensed Abbey's resistance and, for a while, reciprocated by stealing towels, tearing up shoes and furniture, and carrying off whatever Abbey was using the minute she turned her attention from it.

Then one day Abbey noticed a change in Pup's approach. To her astonishment, he began greeting her joyously each time she came home. Whenever she had to feed him he sat for a moment and gazed at her adoringly before he began eating.

Little by little, Pup loved Abbey into a humbling truce. Today, Abbey says that Pup's persistence has taught her a lot about loving her enemies. She says Pup is winning. But don't tell Aaron.[12]

Is there someone you know—perhaps even someone in your own family—who needs an expression of your love, rather than your resistance?

> *But I say unto you, Love your enemies.*
> —MATTHEW 5:44 KJV

WHAT WOULD YOU SAY?

🙪 STANDING IN line with his squad in the Red Army, Taavi had already made up his mind what he was going to say. The officers made their way toward him, interrogating each soldier down the line with the same question: "Are you a Christian?"

"No," came the answer back.

The questioners neared. Taavi never really had any doubt what answer he would give. They asked, "Are you a Christian?" Without flinching, Taavi said in a clear voice, "Yes."

"Then come with us," ordered the commanding officers.

Taavi followed them immediately. The officers said to him, "We are taking you out of combat preparation. You are a Christian and you will not steal, so we will put you in the kitchen." The kitchen was the biggest black-market operation in the Red Army, with the smuggling and illegal sale of food to hungry soldiers. They knew Taavi's presence would reduce the amount of theft.

When you are challenged for your faith, rise up and boldly proclaim the truth. God will be right there with you and will reward you for your faithfulness. 🐟

You are the salt of the earth. . . . You are the light of the world.
—MATTHEW 5:13-14

A DREAM SO FAIR

THIRTY MEN, red-eyed and disheveled, lined up before a judge of the San Francisco police court. It was the regular morning company of "drunks and disorderlies." The momentary disorder that accompanied the bringing in of the prisoners quieted down and a strange thing happened. A strong, clear voice from below began singing: "Last night I lay a sleeping; there came a dream so fair. . . ."

The song continued. The judge paused. He made a quiet inquiry. A former member of a famous opera company known throughout the nation was awaiting trial for forgery. It was he who was singing in his cell.

Meanwhile the song went on, and every man in the line showed emotion. "Jerusalem, Jerusalem! Sing for the night is o'er! Hosanna in the highest!"

In an ecstasy of melody the last words rang out, and then there was silence. The judge looked into the faces of the men before him. No man was fined or sentenced to the workhouse that morning. The song had done more good than punishment could possibly have accomplished. ✒

> [He] *showed me the Holy City, Jerusalem,*
> *coming down out of heaven from God.*
> —REVELATION 21:10

THE DAY'S ACCOMPLISHMENTS

⟅⟆ IN HIS book *The Joy of Working*, motivational speaker and author Denis Waitley wrote:

When you come down to the bottom line, *joy is accepting yourself as you are right now*—an imperfect, changing, growing, and worthwhile person. Realize that liking yourself is not necessarily egotistical. Understand the truth that although we as individuals are not born with equal physical and mental attributes, we are born with equal rights to feel the excitement and joy in believing we deserve the very best in life.

If you scored a victory today, if you won the prize, if you did the right thing, if you moved beyond yourself and extended an act of love and charity to another human being, rejoice in it! Delight in your awareness that the Lord is working in your life, and working *through* your life to reach others.

To delight in the Lord's work isn't pride. It's a form of praise to your Father, who is *proud* of you anytime you succeed according to His principles and design. All the glory goes to Him. It is *because* of Him that we can succeed.

For in him we live, and move, and have our being.
—ACTS 17:28 KJV

HEAVEN'S SPOT REMOVER

✺ "LET IT snow, let it snow, let it snow." That's the cry of school-aged children everywhere when winter weather finally arrives.

Then it happens. You awaken to a virtual winter wonderland. Before long, however, between the snowballs and snowmen, the forts and the angels, every square inch of clean snow has been used up. Patches of dead grass show through where someone dug down deep to roll a snowman's head. The once pristine landscape is now trampled and rutted.

But something magical happens overnight. While you are sleeping, the snow falls again. You look out your window in the morning to find another clean blanket of snow covering all of the previous day's blemishes. All that was ugly is once again beautiful.[13]

Don't despair when what began as a beautiful day turns into something ugly. The God Who turned the humiliation and shame of His Son's death on the cross into the gift of salvation for all who believe in Him, can take the tattered rags of our daily lives and make them like new again every morning. ✎

You are already clean because of the word I have spoken to you.
—JOHN 15:3

CREATOR GOD

❧ WHEN WE see a beautiful piece of art or hear a stirring symphony, we ask, "Who is the artist? Who is the composer?" When we look at the wonders of nature we are often inspired in the same way, "How did this get here? Who made all this?" Nature compels us to think of its Creator.

Dr. Henry Norris Russell, an astronomer at Princeton University, was giving a public lecture on the many galaxies in the universe. He described the

Milky Way as composed of billions of stars, many of them larger than our sun. He went on and described other galaxies much larger than we have ever known.

At the end of the lecture a woman came to him and asked, "If our world is so little, and the universe is so great, can we believe that God pays any attention to us?"

"That depends, madam," he replied, "entirely on how big a God you believe in."

Can you see God in the world around you? How big is He to you?

You are worthy, O Lord, to receive glory and honor and power;
for You created all things, and by Your will they exist and were created.
—REVELATION 4:11 NKJV

After Darkness, Dawn

⁓ THERE WAS once a city worker whose youth had been spent in evil ways. But one night during a revival meeting he was spiritually born anew. Soon after, he ran into one of his old drinking pals. Knowing his friend needed Jesus, he attempted to witness to him about his newly found peace. His friend made fun of him for "turning pious."

"I'll tell you what," said the new Christian, "you know that I am the city lamplighter When I go 'round turning out the lights, I look back, and all the road over which I've been walking is blackness. That's what my past is like."

He went on, "I look on in front, and there's a long row of twinkling lights to guide me. That's what the future is like, since I found Jesus."

"Yes," says the friend, "but by-and-by you get to the last lamp and turn it out, and where are you then?"

"Then," said the Christian, "why, when the last lamp goes out it's dawn, and there ain't no need for lamps when the morning comes."

*But you are a chosen people, a royal priesthood, a holy nation,
a people belonging to God, that you may declare the praises of him
who called you out of darkness into his wonderful light.*
—1 PETER 2:9

REVIEWING THE DAY

❧ IN *YOU Don't Have to Be Blind to See*, Jim Stovall writes:

Your values determine your character, and they set a framework for the choices you make as well as a framework for evaluating your success. In other words, your values provide the framework for self-accountability. . . .

Each night before I go to bed, I review the day I've just lived. I say about various things I've done or said, "That was good. That was great. That wasn't so hot." In appraising my actions and decisions, I'm able to make midcourse corrections as I pursue my goals. In appraising my deeds of a day, I can close my eyes and have a sense of accomplishment, of being one step closer to the fulfillment of my destiny on earth.

Reviewing the day against the criteria of God's Word is a valuable exercise. It allows you to eliminate both regret and pride, and wipe the slate clean for tomorrow's divine handwriting.

Because of the Lord's mercy and compassion, tomorrow holds a new opportunity to move forward in His power and love. ✍

This I recall to my mind, therefore have I hope. It is of the LORD's mercies
that we are not consumed, because his compassions fail not.
—LAMENTATIONS 3:21-22 KJV

A SABBATH

WHEN WAS the last time you gave yourself permission to be "unproductive" and really enjoy some of life's simple pleasures?

Logan Pearsall Smith wrote, "If you are losing your leisure, look out! You may be losing your soul." When we don't take time for leisure or relaxation, when we give our discretionary time away to busyness, we are living in a way that says, "Everything depends upon me and my efforts."[14]

Consequently, God prescribed a day of rest, the Sabbath, to enjoy His creation. It gives us time to reflect and remember all that He has done for us and all that He is. The Sabbath is a time to remember that God is God—and we're not!

The Sabbath doesn't have to be Sunday. You can take a Sabbath rest anytime you relax and turn your focus to God and His creation. Sometimes you have nothing better to do than relax. You may have something *else* to do, but you don't have anything *better* to do.

Relax and just enjoy God's creation. After all, He *created* it for you to enjoy.

> *But be glad and rejoice for ever in that which I create.*
> —ISAIAH 65:18 RSV

71

THE SUNSET DECISION

∂ JENNY LIND won worldwide success as an operatic singer. She sang for heads of state in many nations and thrilled hundreds of thousands of people with her fabulous voice in an era when all performances were live. Yet at the height of her career she left the stage and never returned.

Once an English friend went to visit her. He found her on the beach with a Bible on her knee; her attention was fixed upon a magnificent sunset.

They talked of old days and eventually the conversation turned to her new life. "How is it that you came to abandon the stage at the apex of your career?"

Jenny offered a quiet answer that reflected her peace of heart: "When every day, it made me think less of this (laying a finger on the Bible) and nothing at all of that (pointing to the sunset), what else could I do?"[15]

Nothing in life is as precious as your relationship with your Creator, and in turn, your relationships with others. Ultimate fulfillment comes not in career or money, but in relationship. ✍

But if serving the LORD seems undesirable to you,
then choose for yourselves this day whom you will serve. . . .
But as for me and my household, we will serve the LORD.
—JOSHUA 24:15

LETTING GO

THE SPIDER monkey is a tiny animal native to South and Central America. Quick as lightning, it is a very difficult animal to capture in the wild. However, the best way to catch one is with a pop bottle and a peanut.

How? The spider monkey reaches into the bottle to get the peanut, but he can't get his hand out of the bottle as long as he is clenching the peanut. The spider monkey is too intent on that one peanut to let go. In fact, you could dump a wheelbarrow full of peanuts right next to him, and he wouldn't let go of that peanut.

How many of us are like that? Unwilling to change a habit, be a little flexible, try a new method, or give up something that we know is bringing about our demise? We stubbornly cling to our way, even if it brings pain.

Today, don't cling to a negative situation that may be sapping you of your full vitality, energy, creativity, and enthusiasm for living. As the well-known phrase advises, "Let go, and let God!"

Forgetting those things which are behind, and reaching forth unto those things which are before, I press toward the mark for the prize of the high calling of God in Christ Jesus.
—PHILIPPIANS 3:13-14 KJV

SOLID ROCK

⮞ OF THE more than 100 hymns he wrote, eighteenth-century hymn writer Edward Mote is probably best known for "The Solid Rock." The chorus came to him one morning as he was preparing for work, and he had the first four verses written down before the day was done. The following Sabbath, he stopped to visit a dying parishioner and sang the hymn to her. She was so comforted by it, her husband asked Mote to give him a copy of the hymn. He did, but not before adding two more verses.

My hope is built on nothing less
Than Jesus' blood and righteousness;
I dare not trust the sweetest frame,
But wholly lean on Jesus' name.
On Christ, the solid Rock, I stand—
All other ground is sinking sand,
All other ground is sinking sand.[16]

All of us are building something on this earth, be it a relationship, a career, or a physical structure. Each day we are wise to check our foundation and make sure we're building on the Rock Who will last forever.

See, I lay a stone in Zion, a tested stone,
a precious cornerstone for a sure foundation.
—ISAIAH 28:16

NIGHT LIGHTS

AN ILLINOIS pastor had six couples enrolled in a new-members' class that met on Sunday evenings in one couple's home. The couples enjoyed each other's company and developed a deep sense of commitment to one another.

One night, the pastor received a call from one of the wives in the group. Her husband's plane had gone down, and she didn't know if he was dead or alive. The pastor immediately called the other group members, who rallied around her.

They sat and prayed with her until word came that her husband was dead. Then, various women took turns baby-sitting and staying with her during those first difficult nights.[17]

For many people, this experience would seem like a night without end. But because her friends let their lights shine into her darkness, dispelling the shadow, they reminded her of the God Who understood her pain and promised to see her through it.

In a world that seems to grow darker day by day, let the Lord turn your darkness into light so that you can brighten the lives of those around you. ✍

You are my lamp, O LORD; the LORD turns my darkness into light.
—2 SAMUEL 22:29

RUNNING ON EMPTY

❧ SOME YEARS ago, a research physician made an extensive study of the amount of oxygen a person needs throughout the day. He was able to demonstrate that the average workman, for instance, breathes thirty ounces of oxygen during a day's work, but he uses thirty-one. His body is tired, and he is in oxygen debt. He goes to sleep and breathes more oxygen than he uses to sleep, but in the morning he has regained only five-sixths of the ounce he was short.

The night's rest does not fully balance the day's work!

By the seventh day, then, he is six-sixths of an ounce, or one whole ounce, in debt again. He must rest an entire day to replenish his body's oxygen requirements.

Most people think that "keeping the Sabbath" is solely an act of devotion to God. But in turning your attention to Him, He can offer you true rest and replenishment in every area of your life—spirit, soul, *and* body. He is not only our daily strength, He is our source of rest, recreation, and replenishment.

There remains, then, a Sabbath-rest for the people of God;
for anyone who enters God's rest also rests from his own work,
just as God did from his.
—HEBREWS 4:9-10

LOOKING BACK

WE ALL know the story of the movie, *It's A Wonderful Life*. George Bailey's Uncle Billy loses $8,000 on the day the bank examiner shows up, and George is frantic. In his despair he says, in essence, "I'm a failure at business, my child is sick, our house is all but coming down around our ears—why not just put an end to my life?"

Thank God for Clarence! Through a series of events, this angel without wings shows George how much his life has meant to his family and friends. Without George, Harry Bailey would be dead, Mr. Gower the druggist would be an ex-convict, Mrs. Bailey would be a frightened old maid, and Bedford Falls would be known as Pottersville.

When George Bailey took an honest look back at his life, he could see that despite all the disappointments, there were more than enough triumphs to balance the scales. When George was redeemed—in his own eyes—his younger brother called him "the richest man in town," and in the ways that really counted, he was.

When you are on your beds, search your hearts and be silent.
—PSALM 4:4

FIVE MINUTES

❧ IF YOU wake up as weary as you were when you went to bed the night before, try to recall what you were thinking about the last five minutes before you went to sleep. What you think about in that five minutes impacts how well you sleep.

For example, if those last minutes are spent in worry over the work of the day or the responsibilities of the next day, the subconscious records and categorizes that as fear and acts as if the fear is reality. That fear keeps the body from really resting.

However, if those last five minutes are spent contemplating some great idea, an inspiring verse, or a calm and reassuring thought, it will signal to the nervous system, "All is well," and put the entire body in a relaxed, peaceful state.

Many of your days that begin badly, started out that way the night before, during those critical last five minutes of conscious thought. With intentional effort, you can input positive, healthy thoughts into your conscious mind and pave the way for quiet, restful sleep.

> *In peace I will both lie down and sleep; for thou alone,*
> *O LORD, makest me dwell in safety.*
> —PSALM 4:8 RSV

SERENITY

𝒮𝓊 MANY PEOPLE are familiar with the "Serenity Prayer," although most probably think of it as a prayer to be said during a time of crisis: "God grant me the Serenity to accept the things I cannot change, Courage to change the things I can, and Wisdom to know the difference."

Can there be any better prayer to say at the day's end? Those things which are irreversible or fixed in God's order, we need to let be. True peace of mind comes when we trust that God knows more about any situation than we could possibly know. He can turn any situation from bad to good, in His timing and according to His methods.

At day's end, we must recognize that the Lord's wisdom may not be given to us *before* we sleep, but perhaps *as* we sleep. Many people have reported this to be true—they went to bed having a problem they turned over to God in prayer, and awoke with a solution that, in the morning light, seemed "plain as day."

Ask the Lord to give you serenity tonight! 🕊

> *I have [expectantly] trusted in, leaned on, and relied on*
> *the Lord without wavering and I shall not slide.*
> —PSALM 26:1 AMP

PRINT IT

SOME DAYS we lose our sense of direction and can't seem to get back on track. To ensure this doesn't happen again, or at least not as often, we can take some advice from *National Geographic* photographer Dewitt Jones.

Before he goes out to shoot, Jones knows he has to have a good camera with the right lens. Different lenses give different perspectives.

If there's a problem at work that has you stymied, try looking at it from someone else's point of view.

Another important factor is focus. With a turn of the lens, the whole picture can be razor-sharp.

In our work, we sometimes become so focused on one aspect of a problem, we lose sight of the big picture.[18]

When Dewitt Jones empties his camera at the end of a shoot, he knows he's given it his best shot. If we've looked at our work from the right perspective, stayed focused on what's truly important, and been willing to try something different, we too can look back at our day and say, "Print it."

Be very careful, then, how you live—not as unwise but as wise, making the most of every opportunity.
—EPHESIANS 5:15-16

NIGHT LIGHT

☙ THIS NIGHTTIME prayer by Gregory of Nazianzus can help put your mind and heart at rest before going to sleep:

> Lord Jesus, you are light from eternal lights.
> You have dissolved all spiritual darkness
> And my soul is filled with your brightness.
> Your light makes all things beautiful.
>
> You lit the skies with the sun and the moon.
> You ordered night and day to follow each other peaceably.

And so you made the sun and the moon friends.
May I be friends with all whom I meet.

At night you give rest to our bodies.
By day you spur us on to work.
May I work with diligence and devotion,
That at night my conscience is at peace.

As I lay down on my bed at night,
May your fingers draw down my eyelids.
Lay your hand of blessing on my head
That righteous sleep may descend upon me.[19]

Our Heavenly Father loves us even in the dark times. His greatest desire is for us to let the light of His Son, Jesus, shine through the darkness and dispel the shadows. ❧

In him there is no darkness at all.
—1 JOHN 1:5

HEAVENLY MINDED

❧ "IF YOU read history you will find that the Christians who did most for the present world were just those who thought most of the next," wrote C.S. Lewis in *Mere Christianity*.

Christians are actually citizens of another country—Heaven. Christians are persons whose Father is in Heaven; their treasure and home are in Heaven. As citizens of that other country, they are ambassadors who represent that Kingdom on earth.

What does it mean to be an ambassador?

- An ambassador is a representative.

- An ambassador is a foreigner in the country where he is living.

- An ambassador is only a temporary resident of the country where he is living.

- An ambassador always keeps in mind the one he serves.

- An ambassador will assist those who wish to emigrate to his country.

C. S. Lewis said, "Aim at Heaven and you will get earth 'thrown in'; aim at earth and you will get neither." Turn your thoughts toward Heaven and see how it changes your perspective about your life on earth. ✍

For we are his workmanship, created in Christ Jesus for good works,
which God prepared beforehand, that we should walk in them.
—EPHESIANS 2:10 RSV

ENDLESS LOVE

THE BEAUTIFUL hymn, "O Love That Will Not Let Me Go," was penned by a Scottish minister, George Matheson. It was widely speculated that his sister's wedding reminded him of the great disappointment he had experienced just before he was to have married his college sweetheart. When told of his impending blindness, she is said to have informed him, "I do not wish to be the wife of a blind preacher."

Having experienced rejection from an earthly lover, Matheson wrote of a Heavenly Lover Whose love is eternal and faithful:

O Love that wilt not let me go,
I rest my weary soul on Thee;
I give Thee back the life I owe,
that in Thine ocean depths its flow
may richer, fuller be.

O Light that follow'st all my way,
I yield my flick'ring torch to Thee;
my heart restores its borrowed ray,
that in Thy sunshine's blaze
its day may brighter, fairer be.[20]

The love that first drew you to God is the same love that now surrounds you and will be with you throughout eternity. ❧

I have loved you with an everlasting love;
I have drawn you with loving-kindness.
—JEREMIAH 31:3

WHAT DO YOU WANT?

❧ CHILDREN ARE quick to respond to their environment. Babies immediately cry when they are hungry, thirsty, tired, sick, or wet.

As we grow older, maturity requires us to use discernment in making our wants known. It requires we give way to the needs of others.

The Lord, however, tells us we are wise to always come to Him as little children. While looking directly at a man whom He knew was blind, Jesus asked him, "What do you want Me to do for you?" Without hesitation he replied, "Master, let me receive my sight" (Mark 10:51 AMP).

Jesus could see he was blind, yet He asked him to make a request. God knows what we need "before you ask Him" (Matthew 6:8 AMP). Yet, He says in His Word, "By prayer and petition . . . continue to make your wants known to God" (Philippians 4:6 AMP).

State your requests boldly before the Lord tonight. He'll hear you. He'll respond to you. And perhaps just as importantly, you'll hear yourself and respond in a new way to Him. 🕊

> *I thank You and praise You, O God of my fathers,*
> *Who has given me wisdom and might and has made*
> *known to me now what we desired of You.*
> —DANIEL 2:23 AMP

BEYOND THE SUNSET

VIRGIL P. BROCK told how he wrote the beloved hymn, "Beyond the Sunset:"

This song was born during a conversation at the dinner table, after watching a very unusual sunset at Winona Lake, Indiana, with a blind guest, my cousin Horace Burr, and his wife, Grace. . . . Our blind guest excitedly remarked that he had never seen a more beautiful sunset.

"People are always amazed when you talk about seeing," I told him. "I can see," Horace replied. "I see through other people's eyes, and I think I often see more; I see beyond the sunset."

The phrase "beyond the sunset" and the striking inflection of his voice struck me so forcibly, I began singing the first few measures. "That's beautiful!" his wife interrupted.

The first verse of his beautiful hymn says:

> Beyond the sunset, O blissful morning,
> when with our Savior heav'n is begun.
> Earth's toiling ended, O glorious dawning—
> beyond the sunset when day is done. [21]

Ask the Lord to help you see beyond the sunset of today's immediate problems to the dawn of His solutions.

Now we see but a poor reflection as in a mirror; then we shall see face to face.
Now I know in part; then shall I know fully, even as I am fully known.
—1 CORINTHIANS 13:12

SHINING THROUGH

A LITTLE girl was among a group of people on a guided tour of a great cathedral. As the guide explained the various parts of the structure, the little girl's attention was intently focused on a stained glass window.

For a long time she silently pondered the window, looking up at the various figures in the window. Her face bathed in a rainbow of color as the afternoon sun poured into the transept of the huge cathedral.

As the group was about to move on, she gathered enough courage to ask the tour conductor a question. "Who are those people in that pretty window?"

"Those are the saints," the guide replied.

That night, as the little girl was preparing for bed, she told her mother proudly: "I know who the saints are."

"Oh?" replied the mother.

"They are the people who let the light shine through!"[22]

As Christians, we are called to share the light of Jesus, the Source of light, in a world of darkness. Believers can bring hope and encouragement to others by the light of their lives. 🖋

> *Let your light so shine before men, that they may see*
> *your good works and glorify your Father in heaven.*
> —MATTHEW 5:16 NKJV

FULFILLMENT

❧ FULFILLMENT IS something for which every person seems to long.

For Robert Louis Stevenson, this was the definition of a successful life:

That man is a success who has lived well, laughed often and loved much; who has gained the respect of intelligent men and the love of children; who has filled his niche and accomplished his task; who leaves the world better than he found it, whether by an improved poppy, a perfect poem, or a rescued soul; who never lacked appreciation of earth's beauty or failed to express it; who looked for the best in others and gave the best he had.

Do you have a definition of success against which to gauge your own sense of fulfillment?

There's still time to make today fulfilling. Take a moment to reflect upon your goals, priorities, and values; then ask the Lord to show you where they may need some adjusting. As you rethink these important issues, you will be filled with a sense of Christ's abundance and will realize true fulfillment comes in simply knowing and obeying Him.

> *I have come that they may have life,*
> *and that they may have it more abundantly.*
> —JOHN 10:10 NKJV

UNGODLY FEAR

IN OUR LIVES, it's either "Thy will be done" or "knock on wood." How very sad it must make our Heavenly Father to watch us allow fear to rob us of joy in the wake of the good things He gives us. Still, some people irrationally feel the only way to hold onto the joyful things of life is to "earn" them. They believe if they don't perform certain rituals in life, they risk losing things of value. As a result, those parts of the Christian life that should bring us closer to the heart of

God often end up as rituals performed out of duty.

The Lord desires a life-giving, life-blessing relationship with you—not a relationship rooted in your fear of loss or failure. The "fear of God" does not mean you're "afraid" of God, it means you have respect for God. A respect born out of trust in His love. Turn to Him this evening for life, not merely to avoid disaster. When you do, you'll meet a Heavenly Father Who loves you completely and unconditionally.

> *He said to them, "Why are you troubled,*
> *and why do doubts rise in your minds?"*
> —LUKE 24:38

LIKE A CHILD

❧ WHAT DID Jesus mean when He said we must receive and welcome the kingdom of God as a little child does? Surely He meant we must accept and embrace God's will for our lives—welcoming the Lord's will without debate, without question, without worry or fear, and with a sense of delight, expectation, and eagerness.

Just like a child opening a present, we must anticipate that the kingdom of God is a joyful and wonderful gift to us.

Andrew Gillies has written a lovely poem to describe the childlikeness the

Lord desires to see in us. Let it inspire your own prayer this evening:

> Last night my little boy confessed to me
> Some childish wrong;
> And kneeling at my knee,
> He prayed with tears—
> "Dear God, make me a man like Daddy—
> Wise and strong; I know you can!"
> Then while he slept I knelt beside his bed,
> Confessed my sins,
> And prayed with low-bowed head—
> "O God, make me a child like my child here—
> Pure, guileless,
> Trusting Thee with faith sincere."

Truly I tell you, whoever does not receive and accept and welcome the
kingdom of God like a little child [does] positively shall not enter it at all.
—MARK 10:15 AMP

A HINT OF ETERNITY

↪ ETERNITY, IN human terms, seems mostly a matter of time—or, perhaps more accurately, timelessness. But eternity is more than a measure of time. Things said to be "eternal" have a quality deeper than simple permanence. The benefits of eternal things are not found solely in the hereafter; they provide satisfaction in this life as well.

Daniel Webster once said: "If we work on marble, it will perish; if on brass, time will efface it; if we rear temples, they will crumble into dust; but if we work on immortal souls and imbue them with principles, with the just fear of God and love of our fellowmen, we engrave on those tablets something that will brighten to all eternity."

In building your life, build with God for eternity. In building the church, build to the glory of Christ for the salvation of souls.

Ask the Lord to show you this evening how to make your life and effort count for eternity, and to give you an awareness of eternity as you face every decision and task that tomorrow may bring.

We fix our eyes not on what is seen, but on what is unseen.
For what is seen is temporary, but what is unseen is eternal.
—2 CORINTHIANS 4:18

109

GO GENTLY INTO THE NIGHT

GARRISON KEILLOR has described a gentle life in this way:

What keeps our faith cheerful is the extreme persistence of gentleness and humor. Gentleness is everywhere in daily life, a sign that faith rules through ordinary things: through cooking and small talk, through storytelling, making love, fishing, tending animals and sweet corn and flowers, through sports, music, and books, raising kids—all the places where the gravy soaks in and grace shines through. Even in a time of elephantine vanity and greed, one never has to look far to see the campfires of gentle people. Lacking any other purpose in life, it would be good enough to live for their sake.

We must recognize that gentleness begins within the heart. Gentleness is described in the Scripture as one of the "fruits of the Spirit" (Galatians 5:22-23).

Choose to deal with your family members and friends with gentleness this evening—with kindness, simplicity, and tenderness. In planting seeds of gentleness, you will reap a gentle evening filled with relaxation and rest for your body, mind, and spirit. 🦢

He will feed His flock like a shepherd:
He will gather the lambs in His arm, He will carry them in
His bosom and will gently lead those that have their young.
—Isaiah 40:11 AMP

VITAL CONNECTIONS

❧ THE ROOT system of bunch grass that grows in the hilly high country is deep, far reaching, and very extensive. This sturdy grass withstands the extensive grazing and trampling of livestock. Even so, each year the bunch grass puts out new growth.

All year round the bunch grass provides protein for animals. Even when covered by winter snow, it provides rich nutrition for deer, mountain sheep, and range horses. In the fall, its bronze blades provide one of the best nutrition sources available.

People, too, need vast root systems so their lives can be nourished and so they can provide nourishment for others.

What makes up our root system? For most of us, it's family, friends, coworkers, and people in our church. It's people who have loved us, believed in us, and given us a helping hand as we've struggled to find our place in the world.

Still, as important as all these things are, our most vital connection is to God, the Source of everything that sustains our lives. Let your roots grow down deep into the soil of God's loving presence.[23]

As you received Christ Jesus the Lord, so continue to live in him.
Keep your roots deep in him and have your lives built on him.
—COLOSSIANS 2:6-7 NCV

VALUE FAMILY

❧ THOMAS MOORE once wrote: "Family life is full of major and minor crises—the ups and downs of health, success, and failure in career, marriage, and divorce—and all kinds of characters. It is tied to places and events and histories. With all of these felt details, life etches itself into memory and personality. It's difficult to imagine anything more nourishing to the soul."[24]

We hear a great deal in our society today about family values. *Perhaps the key to family values is to value family!* Make family time a priority. Choose to spend time with your loved ones—not simply quality time, but also a *quantity* of time.

One psychologist has said, "A family is only as sick as the secrets it keeps." Choose to be a healthy family in which there are no secrets and in which the truth is freely spoken with love (see Ephesians 4:15).

After all, you are called to be part of the family of God for all eternity. Isn't now a good time to learn how to be a good family member? 🦋

> *When I think of the wisdom and scope of his plan I fall down on*
> *my knees and pray to the Father of all the great family of God—*
> *some of them already in heaven and some down here on earth.*
> —EPHESIANS 3:14-15 TLB

FORTY WINKS

HAVE YOU ever tried to stay up for more than twenty-four hours? It's a near-impossible feat for most of us. Some scientists believe that sleep-inducing chemicals build up in the brain and eventually knock us out. But with certain jobs (such as being a physician) or round-the-clock responsibilities (such as parenting), some of us are occasionally called upon to pull the graveyard shift. Rested or not, we have to be ready to jump into action at a moment's notice. We *can* do it—especially if we've managed to keep our normal workload and responsibilities within bounds.

In a medical emergency, it takes several people to perform all the ministrations required, and it requires shift work to be sure everyone is rested enough to do their jobs well.

In your times of need, be willing to ask others for help. And above all, seek the help of your Heavenly Father, Who needs no sleep. He is able to watch over you and provide for you every waking—and sleeping—moment.

> *He who keeps you will not slumber. Behold,*
> *He who keeps Israel shall neither slumber nor sleep.*
> —PSALM 121:3-4 NKJV

DISCRETIONARY TIME

AMY WU wrote about her aunt who "tends to her house as if it were her child." Her aunt can afford a housekeeper, but she enjoys doing her own housework.

Amy went on, "I'm a failure at housework. I've chosen to be inept and unlearned at what my aunt has spent so much time perfecting. Up to now, I've thought there were more important things to do."

But those "more important things" didn't turn out to be all that important.

She explained, "It isn't as if we're using the time we save for worthwhile pursuits. . . . Most of my friends spend the extra minutes watching TV, listening to music, shopping, chatting on the phone, or snoozing."

She concluded, "Sure, my generation has all the technological advances at our fingertips. But in the end, we may lose more than we've gained by forgetting the important things in life."[25]

How do you spend your discretionary time—like Amy's friends? Or, is it spent caring for family, growing closer to the Lord, or "getting understanding"? Are you "saving" too much time? ✍

In all your getting, get understanding.
—PROVERBS 4:7 NKJV

HOME FIRES

❧ ERNESTINE SCHUMAN-HEINK is not the first to ask, "What is a home?" But her answer is one of the most beautiful ever penned:

A roof to keep out the rain. Four walls to keep out the wind. Floors to keep out the cold. Yes, but home is more than that. It is the laugh of a baby, the song of a mother, the strength of a father. Warmth of loving hearts, light from happy eyes, kindness, loyalty, comradeship. Home is first school and first church for

120

young ones, where they learn what is right, what is good, and what is kind. Where they go for comfort when they are hurt or sick. Where fathers and mothers are respected and loved. Where children are wanted. Where the simplest food is good enough for kings because it is earned. Where money is not so important as loving-kindness. Where even the tea-kettle sings from happiness. That is home. God bless it.[26]

Good family life is never an accident but an achievement by those who share it. Is your house a home? Love will make it so!

Teach the young women to be sober,
to love their husbands, to love their children.
—TITUS 2:4 KJV

THE DINNER TABLE

WHEN WE reflect upon good times we have shared with family members, our memories often settle upon family meals—not necessarily holiday feasts, but regular family dinnertime food and conversation. When we sit at a table with one another, we not only share time, space, and bread, but in a deeper way, our lives.

Elton Trueblood has written eloquently about family dinnertime. Perhaps it's time we reinstitute this practice in our lives!

122

When we realize how deeply a meal together can be a spiritual and regenerating experience, we can understand something of why our Lord, when he broke bread with his little company toward the end of their earthly fellowship, told them, as often as they did it, to remember him. We, too, seek to be members of his sacred fellowship, and irrespective of what we do about the Eucharist, there is no reason why each family meal should not take on something of the character of a time of memory and hope.

When was the last time your family gathered together for a meal? 🐦

And He took bread, gave thanks and broke it, and gave it to them.
—LUKE 22:19 NKJV

NOTHING'S BITING

❧ ONCE UPON a time, fishing was a survival skill. In modern times, it has become a sport, with fishermen competing to see who can catch the first fish, the largest fish, the orneriest fish, or the most fish.

For Nick Lyons, an avid fisherman, fishing does more than take him away from the noise and confusion of daily life. "Fishing completes me," he says. If he wants to escape to a quiet place, he has only to think back to previous fishing trips.[27]

All of us need a "boat in the middle of the lake" to escape to now and then, at least in a figurative sense. We need a place where we can sit down, throw our lines in the water, and wait patiently for the fish to bite. And if they aren't biting? Who cares? As any avid fisherman will tell you, it's not always about filling your bucket. Sometimes, it's about enjoying the sun on your head, the wind in your face, and the peace that invades your soul. ✍

Where the river flows everything will live.
—EZEKIEL 47:9

RESTING IN THE LORD

HENRY G. BOSCH tells a story about the English steamer *Stella*, which was wrecked on a rocky coast many years ago. Twelve women set out into the dark stormy waters in a lifeboat, and the boisterous sea immediately carried them away from the wreckage.

They probably would have lost all hope if it had not been for the spiritual stamina of one of the ladies, Margaret Williams. Urging her companions to put their trust in the Lord, she encouraged them by singing hymns of comfort.

Early the next morning a small craft came searching for survivors. The man at the helm would have missed the women in the fog if he had not heard Miss Williams singing.

Have you ever had a long sleepless night when the trials and "storms" of the day refuse to leave you? Instead of lying there awash in worry, frustration, fear, or anger, try Miss Williams' method—sing hymns of faith. As you turn your thoughts to the true Rescuer, you are likely to find yourself relaxing in His arms and drifting off to sweet sleep. ✍

He who dwells in the shelter of the Most High
will rest in the shadow of the Almighty.
—PSALM 91:1

FIX YOUR FOCUS

 JAN AND her husband Al had been active in ministry to young couples. They often stayed up long into the night helping families or marriages in crisis.

Jan, however, struggled with chronic medical problems and had reached the point where she could no longer maintain such an active pace. Her doctor advised her, "Let it go, Jan, you can't handle that anymore."

On the outside she did let go, but on the inside she held to the past. During that difficult time, she became friends with a minister who counseled her with the wisdom of his seventy-five years. He told her, "For every look you take at yourself, take ten looks at the Savior. Quit trying to live your own idea of the Christian life. Fix your gaze on Jesus, and He will change you."[28]

Tonight remember, God has a plan for your life. Focus on God and where He wants to take you. Keeping your eyes focused on God will give you hope for the future and bring you closer to the One Who knows the plan.

> *"I know the plans I have for you," declares the LORD,*
> *"plans to prosper you and not to harm you,*
> *plans to give you hope and a future."*
> —JEREMIAH 29:11

THE GUIDING LIGHT

 DR. ALEXANDER of Princeton once described a little glowworm which took a step so small it could hardly be measured. But as it moved across the fields at midnight, there was just enough light in its glow to light up the step ahead. So as it moved forward, it always moved into the light.

At times we face issues that leave us feeling directionless, like we are stumbling around in the dark. However, the Bible says, "The path of the

130

righteous is like the first gleam of dawn, shining ever brighter till the full light of day" (Proverbs 4:18).

The Cathedral of Florence is considered to stand on marshy ground, so the builder left a small opening in the dome through which a shaft of light streams every June 21. The sunbeam should squarely illuminate a brass plate set in the floor of the sanctuary. If it doesn't, it indicates the structure has shifted.[29]

Spend some time reading your Bible tonight. It is God's guiding light to lead you along your path and illuminate your way. ✒

Your word is a lamp to my feet and a light for my path.
—PSALM 119:105

STARGAZING

❧ WHILE VISITING relatives who lived in a rural area, a father decided to take his young daughter for a walk. The family lived in a large city, where evening walks were not the custom. The father could hardly wait to see how his daughter would respond to a star-filled sky.

At first, his daughter was playful, exploring the flowers and insects along the edge of the dirt lane. As dusk turned into night, however, she became a little fearful. She seemed grateful for the flashlight. Suddenly, she looked toward the sky and exclaimed with surprise, "Daddy, somebody drew dots all over the sky!"

When God showed Abraham the stars and asked him to count them, He knew Abraham would not be able to. They are innumerable. The stars are a picture of God's hope for all of us—for you, for your family, for the world. Stargazing is one of the best ways to get your earthly life back into perspective and realize in God's infinite universe, He has a specific plan for you—just as He did for Abraham. ♫

Then He brought him [Abraham] outside and said,
"Look now toward heaven, and count the stars if you are able to
number them." And He said to him, "So shall your descendants be."
—GENESIS 15:5 NKJV

FAMILY DEVOTIONS

BEDTIME PRAYERS are often limited to requiring children to say a little memorized prayer before being "tucked into bed." However, bedtime prayers can become true family devotions if the entire family gathers at the bedside of the child who retires first, and each member of the family says a heartfelt prayer that is spontaneous and unrehearsed. A verse or two of Scripture might be read prior to prayer. The point of such a devotional time is not that a child is "obedient to say a prayer before sleep," but that the child's heart is knit to the heart of God and to the hearts of other family members.

Spontaneous, unrehearsed prayers invite a child to speak freely and openly to the Lord. Having each family member pray allows the child to catch a glimpse of the soul of a brother or sister, or of his mother or father—and to learn from their example how to relate to God, how to give praise, and how to make their requests known to a loving Heavenly Father.

When you pray . . . pray to your Father who is in the secret place;
and your Father who sees in secret will reward you openly.
—MATTHEW 6:6 NKJV

STRANGERS AND PILGRIMS

THE DETAILS of everyday life can cause our attention to be focused on only the "here and now." And when change comes, it can be exciting, bittersweet, or even sad: The birth of a child, the first day of school, the death of a parent.

In his book, *Strangers and Pilgrims*, W. R. Matthews describes how we should see ourselves. While he doesn't recommend a total detachment from the life that swirls around us, he advises:

"We should live in this world as if we did not wholly belong to it and . . . we should avoid that complete absorption in its vicissitudes into which the most eager spirits easily fall. It is wise to remind ourselves that even our most cherished ambitions and interests are passing; the soul will grow out of them or at least must leave them behind."

Home, of course, is Heaven, where we can finally take off our "Visitor" badges and establish a permanent residency. The phases of our earthly existence will no longer apply. The old order of things will be passed away. ℘

There will be no more death or mourning or crying or pain,
for the old order of things has passed away.
—REVELATION 21:4

UNFORGIVENESS

❧ JUST BEFORE Leonardo da Vinci commenced work on his depiction of *The Last Supper*, he had a violent quarrel with a fellow painter. Leonardo was so enraged and bitter that he determined to paint the face of his enemy into the face of Judas, and thus take his revenge by handing the man down to succeeding generations in infamy and scorn.

However, when he attempted to paint the face of Christ, Leonardo could

138

make no progress. At length, he came to the conclusion that the thing that was checking and frustrating him was the fact that he had painted his enemy into the face of Judas.

When he painted out the face of Judas, he commenced anew on the face of Jesus, with the success that has been acclaimed through the ages.

You cannot be painting the features of Christ into your own life, and at the same time, be painting another face with the colors of enmity and hatred. Forgive, and you will be forgiven and set free to do your work and to live your life with inner peace.

For if you forgive men when they sin against you,
your heavenly Father will also forgive you.
—MATTHEW 6:14

THE SMALL STUFF

❧ CLEARING AWAY the small stuff of life can either be regarded as a burden or viewed as paving the way to God's plan and purpose.

This prayer by Mary Stuart reflects a desire to move beyond the small stuff:

Keep me, O Lord, from all pettiness. Let me be large in thought and word and deed.

Let me leave off self-seeking and have done with fault-finding.

Help me put away all pretence, that I may meet my neighbor face to face, without self-pity and without prejudice.

May I never be hasty in my judgments, but generous to all and in all things.

Make me grow calm, serene, and gentle. . . .

Grant that I may realize that it is the trifling things of life that create differences, that in the higher things we are all one.

And, O Lord God, let me not forget to be kind![30]

When we handle the small things, we can move on to the greater things, but what we may not realize is often the small things are great things in disguise! ✒

Thou hast been faithful over a few things, I will make thee ruler over many things: enter thou into the joy of the lord.
—MATTHEW 25:21 KJV

NOTHING TO FEAR

∾ THE WORLD can be a scary place anytime there's darkness caused by the forces of evil. Sometimes we just have to say, "Father, help!"

The story is told of the Patons, who in the nineteenth century, went as missionaries to a forsaken island known for its cannibals and headhunters. In the early part of their ministry, Paton and his wife slept on the beach each night. The natives watched them from nearby bushes but never came near. Thirty fruitful years of ministry later, one of their converts asked Paton, "Those nights you and your wife slept on the beach . . . what was that army we saw surrounding you?" Paton, of course, had no army, but he knew beyond a doubt who the "soldiers" were, and that God had sent them.[31]

The God Who watches over "your going out and your coming in" (Psalm 121:8 NKJV) can be counted on to protect you from the darkness of evil. Trust in His power, His love, and His name to keep you through the night, whatever darkness you may face.

Let him who walks in the dark, who has no light,
trust in the name of the LORD and rely on his God.
—ISAIAH 50:10

FAITHFULNESS

∽ WITH EACH day, there remains a residue of things left undone, unsaid, unachieved, or unconquered.

As you conduct a full review of your day—the bad as well as the good—it may be helpful to recall these words of Annie Johnson Flint in her poem "What God Hath Promised:"

> God hath not promised
> Skies always blue,
> Flower-strewn pathways
> All our lives through;

God hath not promised
Sun without rain,
Joy without sorrow,
Peace without pain.
But God hath promised
Strength for the day,
Rest for the labor,
Light for the way,
Grace for the trials,
Help from above,
Unfailing sympathy,
Undying love.

You may not have been as successful today as you would have liked. But every day you *can* be faithful to the Lord, just as He is faithful to you. Remember the things God *has* promised, and your journey will be easier day by day.

"The LORD is my portion," says my soul, "Therefore I hope in Him!"
—LAMENTATIONS 3:24 NKJV

RITUALS

"RITUAL" REFERS to a system of rites—doing the same thing in the same way, every time. Rites of passage, or rituals, if you will, are common customs—unique, perhaps, to their era but familiar to all.

In keeping with a society that embraces change, a ritual is now looked upon as anything performed on a regular basis. Once a more exalted term, it can now refer to something as mundane as brushing one's teeth. Whether we realize it or not, we all have rituals. The things we do to prepare for work in the morning, and the things we do when we get home each night, are rituals that orient us to the time of day and our location.

Our rituals can bring us peace and comfort, or leave us stuck in a rut. The questions each of us need to ask about our rituals are these: "Do they extend my life? Do they make my life more meaningful?" If the answers are "no," then it's time to reinvent them or find some new ones. ৶

A heart at peace gives life to the body.
—PROVERBS 14:30

NEVER OUT OF SIGHT

 SANDRA PALMER CARR wrote in *The Upper Room* about an incident that happened when one of her sons was a small boy. One day when her son Boyd was four years old, he was sitting on her lap. His knees were bent so he could straddle her lap and sit facing her.

Suddenly, he lifted his head and stared straight at her. He became very still. Then he cupped her face in his little hands and said in a near whisper, "Mommy,

I'm in your eyes."

"We stayed that way for several long moments and the room grew quiet," Sandra wrote. "And I'm in yours," she whispered back to Boyd.

In the days that followed, Boyd checked to see if his discovery had lasted. "Am I still in your eyes, Mommy?" he asked as he reached up to her. As she pulled him close to her, he could see for himself and was reassured.

We are the objects of God's tender care and attention. You can have a grateful and confident heart because you know that you are always in His eyes. 🖋

> *The eyes of the LORD are upon the righteous.*
> —PSALM 34:15 KJV

GOD'S CLOUD OF PROTECTION

❧ NEWSCASTER AND commentator Paul Harvey told radio listeners this remarkable story from World War II:

From the island of Guam, one of our bombers took off for Kokura, Japan. They circled above the cloud that covered the target for half an hour. Then three-quarters of an hour. Then fifty-five minutes. Finally, their gas supply reached the danger point. It seemed a shame to be right over the primary target and then have to pass it up, but there was no choice.

With one more look back, the crew headed for the secondary target. Upon arrival, the sky was clear. "Bombs away!"

Weeks later, an officer received information from military intelligence that thousands of allied prisoners of war had been moved to Kokura a week before the suspended bombing!

The secondary target that day was Nagasaki. The bomb intended for Kokura was the world's second atomic bomb!

Every day, you must make choices. Even when you can't see beyond the circumstances and may be afraid to go on, God *can* see and will lead you in the right path. ✺

> *For this God is our God for ever and ever;*
> *he will be our guide even to the end.*
> —PSALM 48:14

RESTORATION

🕊 IN A REMOTE Swiss village stood a beautiful church. The church was not only beautiful to look at, but it had the most incredible pipe organ in the entire region.

But then a problem arose. The area no longer echoed with the glorious fine-tuned music of the pipe organ.

Musicians and experts from around the world tried to repair the organ. Then one day an old man appeared at the church door. The sexton reluctantly agreed to let the old man try his hand at repairing the organ.

Three days after his arrival, at precisely high noon, the mountain valley once again was filled with glorious music. Everyone in town stopped what they were doing and headed for the church.

After the old man finished his playing, someone asked him how he could have restored the magnificent instrument when even the world's experts could not. "It was I who built this organ fifty years ago." He said, "I created it—and now I have restored it."[32]

God, your Creator, knows exactly what you need. He created you; therefore, He can restore you. ✍

But those who hope in the LORD will renew their strength.
They will soar on wings like eagles; they will run and not grow weary,
they will walk and not be faint.
—ISAIAH 40:31

FINISHING WELL

 As Jesus exhaled His last breath He declared, "It is finished" (John 19:30). It is the moment that marked an end, a finish, but also became the prelude for a "new beginning," at His resurrection.

Ralph Waldo Emerson offered this advice: "Finish every day and be done with it. You have done what you could. Some blunders and absurdities no doubt crept in; forget them as soon as you can. Tomorrow is a new day; begin it well and serenely and with too high a spirit to be cumbered with your old nonsense. This day is all that is good and fair. It is too dear, with its hopes and invitations, to waste a moment on yesterdays."[33]

The God Who began a good work in you, will finish it day by day, and ultimately bring it to completion (Philippians 1:6).

As he had begun, so he would also complete this grace in you.
—2 CORINTHIANS 8:6 NKJV

SMOOTH SAILING

DWIGHT L. MOODY used to tell this story about darkness and light, inspiring nineteenth-century gospel songwriter Philip P. Bliss to pen a beloved hymn on the subject.

There was a terrible storm one night on Lake Erie. The captain of a ship could see the light from a lighthouse, but, not seeing the lower lights of the harbor, he questioned his pilot about their location.

"Yes, sir, this is Cleveland," the pilot said. "The lower lights have gone out, sir."

"Will we make it into the harbor?"

"If we don't, we're lost, sir," the pilot replied.

The pilot did his best, but it wasn't enough. Without the lower lights to guide them in, the ship crashed on the rocks.

Bliss' great hymn, of course, was, "Let the Lower Lights Be Burning."[34]

Jesus Christ said, "I am the light of the world. Whoever follows me will never walk in darkness, but will have the light of life" (John 8:12). If we keep our eyes focused on Jesus, we'll have a safe trip into the harbor.

God is light and in Him is no darkness at all.
—1 JOHN 1:5 NKJV

ENDNOTES

1   *Unto the Hills: A Devotional Treasury*, Billy Graham (Waco, TX: Word Books, 1986), p. 130.

2   Ibid., p. 223.

3   *Spiritual Fitness*, Doris Donnelly (NY: Harper-SanFrancisco, A Division of HarperCollins, 1993), pp. 155-156, 165-166.

4   *The Last Word*, Jamie Buckingham (Plainfield, NJ: Logos International, 1978), pp. 169-170.

5   *Decision*, March 1996, p. 33.

6   *A Moment a Day*, Mary Beckwith and Kathi Mills, ed., (Ventura, CA: Regal Books, 1988), p. 25.

7   "When God Whispers Your Name," Max Lucado, *The Inspirational Study Bible*, Max Lucado, ed. (Dallas, TX: Word, 1995), p. 596.

8   *101 More Hymn Stories*, Kenneth W. Osbeck (Grand Rapids, MI: Kregel Publications, 1985), pp. 24-26.

9   *A Moment a Day*, Mary Beckwith and Kathi Mills, ed. (Ventura, CA: Regal Books, 1988), p. 174.

10 Ibid., p. 184.

11 "No Wonder They Call Him the Savior," Max Lucado, *The Inspirational Study Bible*, Max Lucado, ed. (Dallas, TX: Word, 1995), pp. 635-636.

12 *A Moment a Day*, Mary Beckwith and Kathi Mills, ed. (Ventura, CA: Regal Books, 1988), p. 247.

13 *God Works the Night Shift*, Ron Mehl, (Sisters, OR: Multnomah Books, 1994), pp. 98-100.

14 *Slowing Down in a Speeded Up World*, Adair Lara (Berkeley, CA: Canari Press, 1994), p. 159.

15 *Encyclopedia of 7,700 Illustrations*, Paul Lee Tan, ed. (Garland, TX: Bible Communications Inc., 1979), p. 884.

16 *101 More Hymn Stories*, Kenneth W. Osbeck (Grand Rapids, MI: Kregel Publications, 1985), pp. 274-277.

17 *Decision*, January 1996, pp. 28-29.

[18] *Creative Living*, Autumn 1995, pp. 20-24.

[19] *The HarperCollins Book of Prayers*, Robert Van de Weyer, ed. (NY: HarperSanFrancisco, A Division of HarperCollins, 1993), pp. 175-176.

[20] *Amazing Grace*, Kenneth W. Osbeck (Grand Rapids, MI: Kregel Publications, 1993), p. 49.

[21] Ibid., p. 228.

[22] *Give Your Life a Lift*, Herman W. Gockel (St. Louis, MO: Concordia Publishing House, 1968), pp. 38-39.

[23] *Songs of My Soul: Devotional Thoughts from the Writings of W. Phillip Keller*, Al Bryant, ed. (Dallas, TX: Word Publishing, 1989), p. 95.

[24] *The Treasure Chest*, (San Francisco, CA: HarperSanFrancisco, 1995), p. 93.

[25] *Newsweek*, January 22, 1996, p. 14.

[26] *The Treasury of Inspirational Quotations & Illustrations*, E. Paul Hovey, ed. (Grand Rapids, MI: Baker Books, 1994), p. 168.

[27] *Field and Stream*, Winter 1996, p. 75.

[28] *Decision*, October 1995, pp. 29-30.

[29] *Encyclopedia of 7,700 Illustrations*, Paul Lee Tan, ed. (Garland, TX: Bible Communications, 1979), p. 492.

[30] *The Treasure Chest*, (San Francisco, CA: Harper SanFrancisco, 1995), p. 109.

[31] *God Works the Night Shift*, Ron Mehl (Sisters, OR: Multnomah Books, 1994), pp. 132-133.

[32] *Illustrations Unlimited*, James S. Hewett, ed. (Wheaton, IL: Tyndale House, 1988), pp. 244-245.

[33] *The Treasure Chest*, (San Francisco, CA: Harper-SanFrancisco, 1995), p. 192.

[34] *101 More Hymn Stories*, Kenneth W. Osbeck (Grand Rapids, MI: Kregel Publications, 1985), p. 175.

Additional copies of this book and other titles
in the *Quiet Moments with God* series
are available from your local bookstore.

Breakfast with God, clothbound devotional
Breakfast with God, portable gift edition
Coffee Break with God, clothbound devotional
Coffee Break with God, portable gift edition
Tea Time with God, clothbound devotional
Tea Time with God, portable gift edition
Sunset with God, clothbound devotional

Honor Books
Tulsa, Oklahoma